P9-BIV-743

Joseph Brant

A. Roy Petrie

Fitzhenry & Whiteside Limited

Contents

CAMROSE LUTHERAN COLLEGE
LIBRARY

The Canadians A continuing series

General Editor: Robert Read
Consulting Editor: Roderick Stewart
Designer: Jack Steiner

Petrie, Auldham Roy, 1921-
 Joseph Brant

(The Canadians)

Bibliography: p. 64
ISBN 0-88902-217-8 pa.

1. Brant, Joseph, 1742-1807. 2. Mohawk Indians—Biography.
I. Series.

E99.M8B815   970'.004'97   C78-001307-7

30,639

The Author

*A. Roy Petrie is Superintendent of Operations for the Lincoln County
Board of Education and has written several books for young readers.*

©1978 Fitzhenry & Whiteside Limited
    150 Lesmill Road
    Don Mills, Ontario   M3B 2T5

*No part of this publication may be reproduced in any form, or by any
means, without permission in writing from the publisher.*

Printed and bound in Canada

The Four Chapter 1
Indian Kings

The story of Joseph Brant and the Iroquois people involves the histories of Britain and the United States as well as Canadian history. One event that had a great influence on Brant's life happened in England in 1710, more than thirty years before his birth.

After the deaths of King William and his wife Queen Mary — joint monarchs of England — Mary's sister Anne inherited the throne in 1702. She ruled until her death in 1714.

During her reign, wars over the succession to the Spanish throne raged on both sides of the Atlantic. In Europe, Holland and England were ranged against France and Spain; in North America, French and English met in bloody battles in what was called Queen Anne's War.

Indians fought on both sides of Queen Anne's War but the Iroquois from the Mohawk Valley were the chief supporters of the British. In order to strengthen this alliance, in 1710 four sachems, or chiefs, of the Five Nations Confederacy known as Iroquois paid a state visit to Queen Anne. The English called them "The Four Indian Kings."

"The Four Indian Kings" caused a sensation in London. They were all almost two metres tall, of imposing bearing and splendid physique. They were also impressively dressed. Because the court was still in mourning for Prince George of Denmark, the Queen's husband, the chiefs were fitted out with black breeches, vests and stockings, over which each wore a scarlet cloak trimmed with gold.

The lords and ladies vied with each other in entertaining the visitors. The chiefs visited the Tower of London and St. Paul's Cathedral. They also attended cockfights, bear fights and wrestling matches. They saw *Macbeth* at the Haymarket Theatre. But the huge audience was more

The Four Indian Kings

interested in the chiefs than the play and was not satisfied until the distinguished guests were given seats on the
stage where they could not only see but be seen. At the
end of the play, an actor recited a poem written in their
honour.

London newspapers covered the visit of the Iroquois
thoroughly. Joseph Addison devoted an entire issue of
The Spectator to the Confederacy of the Five Nations.
Richard Steele used his *Tatler* to point out the political
significance of the visit. Queen Anne commissioned
famous artists to paint their portraits which were to
hang in Kensington Palace, her principal London home.

The highlight of their visit, however, was their formal reception by the Queen at the Court of St. James.
They drove there in two golden coaches each drawn by
six sleek black horses and were presented by the Lord
Chamberlain, the Earl of Shrewsbury.

Why is the English court called the Court of St. James?

The Mohawk sachem Gan Ah Joh Hore, an orator of
some reputation, read the address which had been
prepared on behalf of the Confederacy. This document
emphasized the loyalty of the Five Nations, asked for
more help to carry on the war, and for missionaries to
be sent to the People of the Longhouse to teach them
more about Christianity.

Queen Anne received these pledges of friendship with
sincere pleasure and sent the chiefs' request for religious
instruction to the Archbishop of Canterbury, president
of the Society for the Propagation of the Gospel in
Foreign Parts. She also promised to build a chapel in
their territory in America and presented each of the four
sachems with an individually inscribed Bible bound in
rich red leather.

Her promise was fulfilled in 1711 when Queen Anne's
Royal Chapel was built in the Mohawk Valley. The
same year she instructed Robert Hunter, Governor of
New York, to superintend the erection of Fort Hunter
around the chapel. Finally, Queen Anne furnished the
church richly. Her Majesty's coat-of-arms hung over the
door and looked down on the reed organ. Her most precious gift, however, was a double set of communion silver, eight pieces in all, designed by colonial silversmiths.
Each was engraved with the royal coat of arms and bore
the inscription, *The gift of Her Majesty, Queen Anne,*

by the Grace of God, of Great Britain, France, Ireland, and of her plantations in North America, Queen to Her Indian Chapel of Mohawks.

One of the "Four Indian Kings" was the father of Joseph Brant, who continued throughout his lifetime the tradition of friendship between Britain and the Iroquois.

Portrait of Joseph Brant's father, commissioned by Queen Anne from the artist Verelst

Hiawatha And Deganawidah Chapter 2

The Iroquois are a proud and ancient people. It is thought that they were one group of a series of migrant Asian tribes which crossed into North America by the land bridge that existed thousands of years ago over the Bering Strait between Asia and Alaska.

The first Iroquois League was formed in the late sixteenth century and originated from a partnership between a Mohawk chief named Hiawatha and a prophet named Deganawidah, or "Double-Tongue" (a stutterer). This league — the Five Nations — consisted of five self-governing nations: the Mohawks, Senecas, Cayugas, Oneidas, and Onondagas. (In 1722, the Tuscaroras joined the league, which was then known as the Six Nations.)

Some records indicate an even earlier League, formed around 1400.

Unlike other Indian groups, who had aristocracies, in Iroquois society a warrior could become a war chief and even a sachem. The fireside, or family, was the basic unit and women held a unique and powerful place in all aspects of society. They took part in the choosing of chiefs, and had an important voice in councils.

Religion played a central role in the life of every Iroquois and hence in the development of the Confederacy. It recognized both good and evil forces operating in all life, and even in inanimate objects. To help a person choose good over evil, each human being had an *orenda*, or soul. The individual *orenda* was weak but, when united with other *orendas* of the fireside and the clan, made the tribe strong and capable of acting righteously.

According to Iroquoian teaching, Teharonhiawagan, Master of Life and the first human on earth, had commanded all men to live righteously and at peace with one another but his wicked brother persuaded them to do wrong. Teharonhiawagan, however, promised that a leader would come to re-establish good. By the late

These masks were worn by members of the False Face Society. Find out more about the society and the part it played in Iroquois culture and religious practices.

sixteenth century the leader was long overdue. The Iroquois nations were disrupted by blood feuds and disputes over hunting and fishing rights.

Then the leader — Hiawatha — appeared and called a general council of all chiefs to end the bloodshed. His original plan for unification included not only the eventually established Six Nations but also the Hurons, Neutrals and the Susquehanna. While many agreed with his appeal for peace, he was opposed by a cunning Onandaga chief named Ototarho. Although Ototarho was a real human being, he is depicted in folklore as a

An Indian council meeting

monster, the embodiment of evil, with a twisted body, the flippers of a turtle and hair of writhing snakes. He was said to have persecuted Hiawatha by killing all seven of Hiawatha's daughters by witchcraft. Hiawatha had to convert Ototarho to his cause but was unable to do so until he met a remarkable man who believed in his vision of peace and love. This man was Deganawidah.

Deganawidah was the son of an unmarried girl who, because of her disgrace, lived with her mother on the outskirts of a Huron village. One night mother and daughter both dreamed that this child would become a great thinker but that he was destined to contribute to the destruction of the Huron nation. Frightened by this prophecy, they tried to destroy the baby by pushing him through a hole they had cut in the ice on a stream. Miraculously he did not die, even though they made two attempts to kill him. Reluctantly they raised the boy, who grew into a withdrawn, reflective man, rejected by his own tribe possibly because of the circumstances of his birth or because of his inability to speak without stammering severely.

Deganawidah, however, had a beautiful face which reflected the soul of a mystic. One day he, too, had a vision. He dreamed of an eagle straddling a strong tree with five powerful roots growing from soil rich with the three ideals of life: soundness of mind and conduct; justice for all; and military power for self-defence and the maintenance and increase of spiritual power. The five roots which fed on these principles were the five original Iroquois nations whose duty was to extend these truths to all humanity. The eagle was a lookout for enemies who might disturb the peace.

Deganawidah left his tribe and wandered south where he met Hiawatha. Hiawatha provided the voice and showed the statesmanship which Deganawidah's stammer had prevented him from expressing. Together they convinced the tribes and even won over Ototarho and the Onondagas.

Out of this understanding grew the Iroquois Confederacy. Its symbol was a tall pine tree, which they called the Tree of Peace. Fifty sachems of unblemished character were appointed for life; only misconduct could demote them. At least every five years, an Onondaga chief who always took the name Ototarho presided over a council of fourteen Onondagas, ten Cayugas, nine Mohawks, nine Oneidas, and eight Senecas to decide all matters concerning the Confederacy.

Other tribes, including the Hurons, decided not to join the Great Peace and after the deaths of Hiawatha and Deganawidah, the Iroquois began with religious fervour to try to convert their neighbours by force.

The Young Warrior Chapter 3

Before the British and the French came to North America, the Iroquois had explored and lived in most of Canada and a large part of the Eastern United States. Evidence of their presence remains in many place names; for instance, "Ontario" and "Canada" are both Iroquois words.

One of their ancestral homes was the Mohawk Valley. The Mohawk River is a tributary of the Hudson River and with its numerous branches provides an almost continuous waterway from Oswego on Lake Ontario to New York City and the Atlantic Ocean. The river flows through beautiful hilly and forested country which even today is serene and peaceful.

Find some other place names which originate from Indian words.

The lands of the Six Nations

The Iroquois nations' first contacts with Europeans were not friendly ones. Samuel de Champlain made permanent enemies of the Iroquois by slaughtering them in battle in 1609. The French troops used muskets, which were unknown to the Indians at that time. Later, Louis XIV made matters worse by offering rewards to anyone who killed or captured an Iroquois. The French allied themselves with the Algonquins, however; colonists on both sides knew they needed the help of native people to find the inland routes along which the fur trade travelled.

When the English arrived, conquered the early Dutch settlers, and began spreading their settlements inland, they ran into opposition from the French. However, the English took advantage of the bad relations between the French and the Six Nations to ally themselves with the Iroquois. A treaty was signed at Albany in 1664. The struggle for control of the American interior was on: on one side, the Iroquois and the British; on the other, the French, the Algonquin, and the Huron, who were enemies of the Iroquois since they had rejected Hiawatha's invitation to join the Confederacy.

By this time, the Six Nations had penetrated far to the west. Strong ties existed between the Mohawks and the Miamis and there were particularly strong bonds with the Wyandots. It became customary for the Mohawks to travel hundreds of kilometres into Wyandot country during the hunting season and remain with their friends for long periods.

In 1742, while his parents were on one of these expeditions in what is today the State of Ohio, Joseph Brant was born. His father, Tehowaghwengarahkwin, was a Mohawk sachem of the Wolf clan whose home was Canajoharie Castle, the central village of three in their native Mohawk Valley. The child was named Thayendanegea ("Two Sticks of Wood Bound Together for Strength").

Tehwaghwengarahkwin (one of the sachems presented to Queen Anne in 1710) died shortly after the birth of his son. His widow then married another Mohawk called Carrihago or "News Carrier," whose Christian name was Barnet or Bernard, which by contraction became Brant. Young Thayendanegea, whose Christian name was Joseph, became known as Brant's Joseph, and in the process of time, Joseph Brant.

One of the major influences on Joseph Brant's future was a man named William Johnson. While Brant was growing up, Johnson was establishing himself as a central force in the Mohawk Valley.

William Johnson was born in Ireland in 1715. His uncle, Sir Peter Warren, an officer in the Royal Navy, purchased an extensive tract of land in the Mohawk Valley in 1735, and two years later sent his young nephew to the colony of New York to oversee the development of his holdings.

Sir Peter's estates, known as Warrenbush, lay south of the Mohawk River and just east of Schoharie Creek.

Sir William Johnson

Here, William Johnson built his first home and engaged in trade with the Mohawk Indians. In 1739, he married Catherine Weissenberg, a German immigrant by whom he had three children.

Through extensive and continual contact with various Indian nations, and by fair and just dealings with them, he came to possess an unusually wide knowledge of Indian affairs, customs and ways of life.

As he prospered he bought additional land. He built four houses in all. His third, constructed in 1749, he called Fort Johnson. The walls of the house were more than half a metre thick and it was surrounded by a stockade. In the roof were two trap doors where sentries could survey the rear of the house and its approaches. Later he built Johnson Hall, his home for the rest of his life.

In 1751, he was sworn in as a member of the Governor's

Fort Johnson, which is now a museum

Council of the Province of New York, and in 1756 he was appointed Superintendent of Indian Affairs.

In 1759, his wife died and he married Joseph Brant's sister, Molly, according to Indian rites. They were to have eight children. Joseph Brant became part of William Johnson's household.

In spite of the various treaties that officially signalled the end of the Anglo-French wars of the mid-eighteenth century in North America, they were little more than truces and there was no peace. When Brant was still a boy, Britain and the colonies were engaged in what Americans call the French and Indian Wars, which culminated in the Seven Years' War (1756-1763).

What other famous battle was fought in Canada in 1759?

In 1755, the thirteen-year-old Brant had accompanied the Mohawk warriors under William Johnson into battle with the French at Lake George. The resulting British

A sitting room at Fort Johnson

victory laid the foundation of Johnson's military fame. He was rewarded with a baronetcy.

Brant, who was in the forefront of the fighting, suffered the terrors of a first battle. He later recalled: "I was seized with such a tremor when the firing began that I was obliged to take hold of a small sapling to steady myself but after the discharge of a few volleys, I recovered the use of my limbs and the composure of my mind."

That Brant quickly overcame this initial fear is attested to by his later reputation as a brave man and a soldier by nature. He confessed in later life: "I like the music of the harpsichord well, and the organ better, but I like the drum and trumpet best of all for they make my heart beat quick."

In 1757, Brant was commissioned as a captain in His Majesty's Royal American Regiment. He accompanied Sir William again during the campaign to capture Oswego, Miami, Duquesne (later Fort Pitt) and Detroit, built by the French along the Great Lakes and the Mississippi to protect the route to Louisiana and prevent the westward expansion of the British American colonies.

The British under General John Prideaux besieged Fort Niagara and Sir William became commanding officer

A plan of Fort Oswego. What strikes you as unusual in the layout of this fort?

following the accidental death of the General shortly after the siege began. On July 24, Captain Charles-Philippe D'Aubrey, who later became governor of Louisiana, approached the fortress with a combined French and Indian force to attempt to raise the siege. Sir William and his Indian allies were prepared for them. In a severe engagement in the open field, British and colonial arms prevailed. The French broke rank and D'Aubrey and most of his officers were captured.

The next day Sir William and the Six Nations acted so vigorously and decisively that the fort was taken with all its military supplies and about 600 prisoners. The loss severed the French lifeline to Louisiana. Young Joseph Brant acquitted himself with distinction in the hard battle for Fort Niagara.

Fort Niagara after its capture by the British and their Indian allies. Although the artist is unknown, tradition has it that he was Sir William Johnson.

Chapter 4 A Different Culture

Brant was well educated at a time when formal education was hard to come by. In addition to his training as a soldier, he was sent to the village school and later to a school for Indian students at Fort Hunter. Scarcely had he returned from the Niagara campaign when a great opportunity came his way. David Fowler, an Indian teacher from the Moor Charity School in Lebanon, Connecticut, came to Sir William Johnson and invited him to send some of the more promising Indian youths to the school. Joseph Brant was among those selected.

Some historians think Brant arrived at Moor's school in 1759. Why do you think it is difficult to be sure of the date?

The school, named after settler Joshua Moor who had donated the land on which it was built, was established by a Congregationalist minister, the Reverend Doctor Eleazer Wheelock. Endowed by Lord Dartmouth and others, it was to become Dartmouth College, with Dr. Wheelock as its president.

Wheelock, the son of a prosperous farmer, was a scholar and an above-average teacher. He was a dignified, handsome man of middle height, with a beautiful speaking voice. Such a man could not fail to influence his pupils.

Brant was nineteen when he arrived at the school in 1761 and older than several of the other new students. He wore a suit of fine deerskin made by his mother. His two younger Mohawk companions wore only breech-cloths and moccasins. "The other [Brant] being of a family of distinction, was considerably clothed, Indian fashion, and could speak a few words of English," wrote Dr. Wheelock.

Brant was disappointed with the appearance of the school; he had expected something quite impressive. It consisted of a simple, good-sized house with a smaller one beside it. David Fowler, who had accompanied the new students to the school, showed them the chapel, a spacious room on the ground floor equipped with rows of benches and a pulpit, and a smaller room which was

Dr. Eleazer Wheelock, when president of Dartmouth College

Dr. Wheeler's study. Upstairs was the dormitory where the students slept. Brant felt an obligation to set an example to the younger boys, but everything was strange and it was several days before he became accustomed to the softness of a bed and was able to sleep.

Each school day began and ended with prayers. During his two years at the school Brant studied English and mathematics, some Latin and Greek, and also had many practical lessons in farming. The school owned about ninety hectares of land, and part of the training was intended to wean the Indians away from hunting and give them some expertise in European-style agriculture.

How did schooling in Brant's time differ from today's?

The Indians objected to farm chores, which they regard-
ed as woman's work. Brant didn't enjoy them but he
persevered.

Learning English wasn't easy. All the students were
handed a flat piece of wood shaped like a hand mirror.
On it, under a transparent sheet of horn, was a piece of
paper with rows of odd-shaped black marks. David
Fowler explained that this was called a hornbook and
that the black marks were the English alphabet.

This hornbook dates from about 1780. It is hand painted—the alphabet in red, the numerals in black—and is set in a case of strong brown leather. The hornbook measures approximately 10 cm by 6 cm.

Each student was given a copybook, a quill pen and an ink pot and told to copy the letters from the hornbook. Brant began by awkwardly trying to hold the quill and laboriously tracing the alphabet over and over again. Gradually he saw that he was making progress. Soon he started to read. His textbook was the *New England Primer*. Each letter of the alphabet was illustrated by a verse with a scriptural reference. Haltingly, he read:

"In Adam's fall,
We sin-ned all"

and so on, down to

"Zacchaeus, he
Did climb a tree
His Lord to see."

All the students were required to attend the headmaster's classes in Bible study and the Catechism. During these sessions Brant's attentiveness and intelligent questions caught Dr. Wheelock's attention. "Joseph is indeed an excellent youth, he has much endeared himself to me, as well as to his master, and everybody also by his good behaviour."

Brant justified his principal's good opinion of his intelligence and dedication. Before he left the school in 1763, he had become competent enough to be an instructor and was baptized as a Christian, a step which was to have a marked effect on the rest of his life. Six years later he was to assist the Reverend Dr. John Ogilvie, a missionary to the Mohawks, in revising, extending, and reprinting the Mohawk Prayer Book.

Chapter 5 **Pontiac's War**

Joseph Brant had not finished his schooling when war broke out again and he returned home.

In 1763, Pontiac, a great chief of the Ottawas, led an uprising of the Indians in the West that developed into a savage war. Pontiac and the chiefs who sided with him were determined to regain the territory acquired by the British after their conquest of the French four years previously. They saw clearly that the expansion of Europeans westward would not only immediately deprive them of their hunting grounds, but would also inevitably ruin their way of life.

Pontiac won 36 western chiefs to his cause and led them against Detroit and other British forts. Urged on by the French, his former allies, Pontiac was at first successful. He burned Fort Sandusky, on Lake Erie, and captured Fort St. Joseph, Fort Miami, Fort Presqu'Isle and other posts. He selected Detroit for his personal attention because it was the key to the upper lakes as well as the tributaries leading to the Mississippi.

Detroit, held by Major Henry Gladwyn, had warning from an Ottawa Indian of the impending attack, and met Pontiac fully armed. Nevertheless, Pontiac kept the fort under siege for six months. A merchant named Jacques Baby smuggled in enough stores to supply the garrison for several weeks.

One supply convoy sent later from Fort Schlosser was captured, but some of the crew escaped and made their way back to Niagara. They returned to Detroit with supplies and troops. On their arrival most of the men were concealed below deck and Pontiac's men were lured into attacking the ship. About three hundred and fifty came at it in their war canoes expecting an easy victory. When the Indians were only a few metres away, a signal brought fifty men to the decks. They swept the surrounding waters with swivel guns and musketry. In minutes, fourteen Indians were killed and scores wounded. The survivors swam ashore from their shattered and sinking canoes. The schooner sailed safely on to disembark fifty men and 150 barrels of provisions and ammunition. Brant is believed to have been among the troops that came to Major Gladwyn's help.

At Michilimackinac, the Indians took the fort by a trick. They were supposedly celebrating the King's birthday on June 4 by playing a game of lacrosse outside the gate. Suddenly the ball was thrown through the gate and the warriors pursued it. Once inside, they fell upon the garrison and overcame everyone within their reach. Using this victory as a lure, Pontiac tried to persuade the Six Nations to join him. They were strongly tempted and this conflict of loyalties created tension in the Confederacy.

Can you name another famous battle in history that was won by a trick?

Eventually the British were able to organize their forces and Sir William Johnson, helped by Brant's increasing influence and reputation, persuaded the Iroquois not to join forces with Pontiac. (Some Senecas had already thrown in their lot with the western tribes.) Brant pointed out the lack of French success against the British, reminded them of their oath of allegiance to the king, and emphasized the fact that Pontiac was losing his Indian allies. Reluctantly the Iroquois Council agreed to continue to support the British.

But Brant was not satisfied merely to neutralize the influence of Pontiac; he took to the field against him. Through his influence and with his aid, Captain Montour, of mixed French and Indian blood, marched westward

The ominous game of lacrosse at Fort Michilimackinac

with 200 Tuscaroras and Oneidas. Near the main branch of the Susquehanna River, they surprised 40 Delawares and made prisoners of the entire party.

A few weeks later a number of Mohawks led by Joseph Brant put another band of Delawares to flight, killed their chief, and took three prisoners. These attacks by the Iroquois disheartened the Shawnees and Delawares and alarmed the Senecas, who had sided with Pontiac to protect their own territory.

A letter from Sir William Johnson to Dr. Wheelock refers to Brant's activities: "Joseph is just returned from an expedition against the enemy who have abandoned their towns, three of which have been burned and four villages consisting in all of about two hundred houses, built with squared logs and containing vast quantities of corn and other supplies, captured. Parties are now in pursuit of the enemy."

How did Pontiac die?

In the autumn of 1763, when the British were able to come to the aid of Detroit, Pontiac sued for peace and the siege was over. Although this virtually ended the rebellion, peace was not finalized until 1768. In that year the British sent two representatives, of whom Sir William Johnson was one, to negotiate with the Indians assembled at Fort Stanwix on the Mohawk River. The proceedings were sweetened by twenty boatloads of presents and concluded with the Treaty of Fort Stanwix. Under the terms of this treaty, the Indians agreed to renounce their claims to the western lands north of the Ohio River, in what is now New York State, and the British secured a stable situation. Joseph Brant returned home to the Mohawk Valley in the spring of 1768.

The American Chapter 6
Revolution

Brant married three times. Shortly after the Pontiac War
he married an Oneida girl, Owaisa, who had helped him
in his negotiations to keep the Oneidas out of an alliance
with Pontiac. She was said to have a terrible temper.
She and Brant had two children, Isaac and Christine.
They lived in a frame house on a farm of 40 hectares,
where they raised horses and cattle. After seven years of
marriage, Owaisa died of tuberculosis.

Isaac loved his mother dearly, and he had inherited
her tempestuous nature. He blamed her illness and death
on Brant, and grew to hate his father. For the sake of his
children, Brant wanted to marry Owaisa's half-sister
Onogala. Anglican church law, however, prohibited
marriage to a deceased wife's sister, so they were married by a more obliging German pastor. Unfortunately,
Onogala also contracted tuberculosis and died within a
year.

Brant remained single until 1775, when he married
Catherine, the daughter of an Irish trader, George
Croghan, and a Mohawk woman. Catherine's temper
made Owaisa's seem lamblike. Brant could not resist
her, nor she him.

In the same year the American Revolution broke out.
The conflict between Britain and the American colonists
had been brewing for some years: the wars with France
had proved costly and Britain looked to the colonies to
help cover the expense. But the Americans were in no
mood to pay taxes without having any say in the decision. They argued that Britain had no right to impose
tariffs when not a single American sat in the British
parliament. Their rallying cry was: "No taxation without
representation."

Not all Americans thought alike about breaking with
the mother country. While some went all out for independence, others remained loyal to Britain. In the same

Sir John Johnson

Sir William Johnson meets the chiefs of an Indian council outside Fort Johnson.

way, the war caused dissension among the Iroquois, who were divided in their allegiance. The British King was a remote leader whom few of the Iroquois had ever seen; their natural sympathies were with the colonists, with whom they lived as neighbours. Only the influence of Sir William Johnson kept them in the British camp.

At this crucial time, Sir William suffered a stroke and died. He had spent the last day of his life exhorting an Indian council of some 500 persons to remain true to the King. His last words to Brant were, "Control your people."

Sir William's son John, who inherited the title and estates, had neither his father's talents nor his charm, so his nephew, Colonel Guy Johnson, took over his duties as superintendent. Brant, by now the war leader of the Six Nations, agreed to be Colonel Johnson's secretary in dealing with Indian affairs. They needed all their combined skills and persuasion, since the grievances of the colonists were real and convincing. As it happened, the Continental Congress (the first governing assembly of the united colonies) blundered in sending only minor officials to treat with Brant and the Iroquois. This insult proved decisive in keeping the Iroquois on the side of Britain.

Most of the colonists in the Mohawk Valley were

pacifist Germans who were personally indebted to the Johnsons and therefore remained loyal to Britain. In fact, the percentage of Tories (Loyalists) was probably higher in the valley than in any other part of the area. Nevertheless, a civil war which pits brother against brother is always bitter and this struggle had all the signs of becoming long and vicious.

While the American colonists fumbled their chances of winning over the Iroquois Confederacy, Brant was being wooed by the highest officials in British North America and in England. In 1774, he and other Indian chiefs had been called to Montreal for consultation with Sir Guy Carleton, Governor of the province of Quebec. Carleton was well aware of Brant's pre-eminence among the Iroquois and the powerful influence he could wield; for his part, Brant worried about the future of his people if the British lost the war.

Sir Guy Carleton, later Baron Dorchester

Everything was done to impress Brant. Major-General Frederick Haldimand, the Commander-in-Chief, was at Montreal, with his entire army deployed on the plain. Brant, in all his campaigns, had never seen so many redcoats.

The military ceremonies over, the council was convened. Carleton reminded the chiefs of their long friendship and alliance with King George III. "I expect you to continue your adherence to the King, and not break the solemn agreement made by your forefathers..." Then Haldimand addressed the meeting and promised, whatever the outcome of the impending struggle, that the Iroquois would lose none of their lands.

When it was Brant's turn to speak, he thanked the British for their promise and assured his hosts that 3000 Iroquois fighting men would join the redcoats in their struggle.

But Guy Johnson was not satisfied; he wanted to speak to King George himself, and Carleton allowed him to take Brant with him to London. Also in the party which travelled to England in 1775 were Brant's cousin John Deseronto and his friend Ohranta.

London overwhelmed the visitors and made Montreal seem a mere village by comparison. The dome of St. Paul's loomed above them and they were impressed by other magnificent buildings, and the great numbers of people. In the streets crowds followed the Indian party everywhere. Brant bought a gold ring inscribed with both his English and Indian name: *J. Brant - Thayendanegea*, which he always wore. The ring was intended as a means of identification if he was killed in battle.

King George gave him two audiences. The first was informal and took place at Kew Gardens, the Royal Family's country home. On this occasion the King presented Brant with a brace of pistols. Brant was surprised to find the King quite an ordinary man and not the godlike person he had expected.

The second visit was formal. Colonel Johnson and Brant, accompanied by Lord George Germain, Secretary of State for the Colonies, drove to St. James Palace in a state coach. There they were ushered into a magnificent throne room. The walls and floor were hung and carpeted in scarlet and George III, in robes of velvet and

King George III, caricatured by the famous James Gilray. To enjoy the work of a great Canadian caricaturist, look at J.W. Bengough's A Caricature History of Canadian Politics.

ermine, sat on a heavy throne on a dais under a canopy emblazoned with the royal coat of arms. Next to him sat Queen Charlotte. Brant was surprised to see Guy Johnson kneel and kiss the King's hand. When the King offered Brant his hand, it was brusquely swept aside, Brant declaring that he kissed the hand of no man. The situation was saved when he gallantly added that he would gladly kiss the Queen's hand.

Brant then assured the King of the continued affection and allegiance of his Indian subjects. King George gave him a gold watch as a token of his appreciation and a silver gorget to mark his commission as a full captain in the British Army. More important to Brant, he promised "the losses [to the Indians] already certified by the Superintendent-General shall be made good."

Brant's visit to London was a triumph. He was toasted
by a British commander as "His Majesty's greatest North
American subject." James Boswell interviewed him for an
article which appeared in the *London Magazine* in July
1776 and George Romney painted his portrait in full Indian
regalia.

Brant and Deseronto were each given a London rifle
as a parting present, and the delegation sailed from
Portsmouth on May 30, 1776 aboard the *Harriot*. Their
return voyage, which had gone quite quietly, was suddenly disrupted by the breaking out of yards of canvas
which quickly caught the breeze. The *Harriot* heeled
heavily but righted herself. Startled, Brant and his
cousin saw a Yankee privateer swiftly bearing down on
them. Hardly had they turned to look when a shot
whistled overhead, rending the canvas and bringing
down splintered timber about their ears.

The captain was bellowing orders to clear away the
smashed masts and canvas, and while the sailors were
struggling to do so, Brant and Deseronto took up posi-
tions on the poop deck and decided to try their new
rifles. Deseronto loaded and directed the fire, while
Brant aimed at the officer directing the privateer's gun-
ners. A sharp report rang out and the officer toppled
from view. Another loaded rifle was passed up and the
same process repeated. In all, they picked off five of the
enemy. Suddenly the privateer veered off and the *Harriot* was left to lick her wounds and limp into New York
and safe haven.

In New York, Brant was met by his former teacher,
Dr. Wheelock, who had joined the rebel cause. Wheelock made a last effort to bring Brant and the Iroquois
over to the American side, but Brant held firm. He
reminded his teacher that it was at Moor's School that
he had been taught "to fear God and honour the King."
He added, "This I propose to do."

The Romney portrait of Brant

Chapter 7 The Scourge of Cherry Valley

By the time Brant had returned from Britain the opening
battles of the American Revolution in Massachusetts
were over. Much of the action was now along the Atlantic coast, but Brant would make his effort felt on the
borders of New York and Pennsylvania, particularly in
the Mohawk Valley, where bitter fighting occurred.

The first of these engagements took place in 1777,
when Loyalist forces set out to capture Fort Stanwix.
The expedition included Brant, as war chief of the
Mohawks and therefore the leader of the Indians who
accompanied Colonel Johnson's Royal Greens, Sir John
Johnson's Rangers, and Colonel John Butler and his
famous Butler's Rangers. They had found unexpectedly
heavy resistance from the garrison, and the siege became
a prolonged one.

After three weeks, a column was sent under General
Nicholas Herkimer, one of the revolutionary com-
manders, to try to relieve the garrison. Herkimer first
hoped to frighten off the Iroquois forces by murdering
Brant. He asked Brant to meet him for negotiations, and
hid several sharpshooters near the meeting site who were
to kill Brant if he refused to surrender the fort. Brant,
however, was suspicious and brought several hundred of
his own men whom he likewise concealed in the surrounding forest. Herkimer's uneasy manner made Brant
even more suspicious, and Joseph gave a shout which
brought his men running. Needless to say, nothing came
of the "negotiations," and both sides prepared for battle.

The British forces set an ambush for Herkimer. The
spot selected by Brant was excellent, on the high ground
west of the ravine through which ran Oriskany Creek.
The bottom of the ravine was marshy and the road
crossed it by means of a causeway.

The Loyalists and their Indian allies formed a semi-
circle with a narrow opening into which the ill-starred

Johnson's Orderly Book.   3

2 Sergts, 2 Corporals, 1 Drumr & 15 Privates.
The Kings' Royal Regt of New York to hold
themselves in Readiness to leave this Quarter
Immediately.

    1776 7th Nov. *P.* Lachine. *C.* Point Clair.
Major Gray.[1] Capts Brown & Delly, with their
Compns to march off Immediately to Point Clair
& to be Quartered as follows : The Major &
Capt Delly, with their Companies at Point Clair
& Capt Brown With a Detachment of a Sergt
and ten from the Cols Compy, a Corporal & 4
Men from Capt Watts and Capt McDonald's
Comps to be at St. Anns, the Cols Comps and
Capt Watts, together with the Staff to be Quartered in the Parish of Lachine in the following
manner. The (lower) Capt Watt's in the Upper
parts of the Parish of Lachine. For Guard to-
morrow 1 S. 1 C. & 9 men. Compns duty 1 S.
1 C. 5 P.

                    Lachine.[2]
1776 8th November. *P.* McLou. *C.* Phil-

A page from the orderly book (military diary) of Colonel Sir John Johnson. Originally written by hand, it was printed in the nineteenth century. What is the difference between an orderly book and a logbook?

colonists marched. The plan worked to perfection and
the whole of Herkimer's army except the rearguard
walked into the trap. Immediately the Americans were
encircled by gunfire and the gap closed behind them.
Almost at once General Herkimer had his horse shot
from under him and his leg severely smashed below the
knee by a musket ball.

    At first it looked as though the trapped forces would
be annihilated, as the enemy seemed behind every rock
and tree. Herkimer, however, had his men sit him down
with his back to a tree, lit his pipe and formed his
troops into defensive circles. He was thus able to fend
off the attacks with bayonets and musketry.

    The battle lasted for more than an hour, with heavy
losses to both sides. Eventually the British forces, seeing
the tenacity of the Americans and hearing more firing

from the fort, withdrew from the field. They claimed the victory. The American forces lost more than 400 men and General Herkimer died shortly afterwards from the amputation of his shattered leg.

The following year, 1778, the incursions of the (Johnson's, Queenstown and Butler's) Rangers and Brant's forces became even more frequent. One occurred at Wyoming in July. Casualties were heavy; many died of wounds suffered in the raid and others drowned in the swamp while fleeing from the enemy. Farmers and their families were killed, and Brant was blamed for cruelty and inhumanity. It was later proven that he was not present at Wyoming.

He was present, although not in command, during an invasion of Cherry Valley late in the same year. During this sortie 34 civilians and 12 soldiers were killed, among them Colonel Alden, commander of the fort. The fort was not taken, however. Here the Senecas did take violent action; many settlers were slaughtered, buildings and the land itself were burned and ruined.

Brant came upon one woman engaged in her household chores, and asked her why she had not fled.

"We are the King's people," she replied.

Brant told her bluntly that this was no protection. At that moment he noticed the Senecas approaching. He quickly told the woman to get into bed and pretend she was sick. She obeyed and the ruse succeeded.

The commander of the Cherry Valley expedition was Captain Walter Butler, who had persuaded his father to lend him some of the Rangers. At first there was no love lost between him and Brant. Brant did not care to serve under a man so much less experienced than himself, but in the interests of their common cause, he resolved not to feud with Butler. Young Butler almost certainly had a personal motive for the campaign; he was seeking revenge for the harsh treatment he had received when imprisoned by the colonists the previous year, and he did nothing to check his men's excesses. But his father was grieved when he heard of his son's irresponsible behaviour in Cherry Valley.

Other raids took place in the Susquehanna Valley in Pennsylvania and the Schoharie Valley of New York. Settlers were murdered, crops burned and cattle driven away. One of the worst incidents was at German Flatts. The preliminary attack by a small party led by Brant himself was upon Andrustown, a secluded hamlet about ten kilometres southeast of German Flatts. This village consisted of seven affluent families who owned a large tract of land. Plunder was the object of the raid. Everything of value that could be removed was carried away. The settlement was then reduced to ashes.

The next target was German Flatts itself. It extended over the richest, most beautiful section of the Mohawk Valley, including the broad alluvial lands beyond the junction of the West Canada Creek and the river and about 16 kilometres of the valley from east to west. In the centre was a fortified stone house called Fort Herkimer. About 70 smaller houses stood on both sides of the valley. The entire settlement was laid waste.

How are alluvial lands formed? What makes them good for farming?

Though there was great destruction of property, the loss of life at German Flatts was small. This was due to Brant's humanity, contrary to the reputation he had acquired through no fault of his own. Like all soldiers, Brant knew that war means extreme violence, but he did the best he could to stop needless bloodshed and cruelty.

Chapter 8 The Clinton-Sullivan Expedition

Revenge by the colonists came the following year. The plan of attack was that one division under General James Clinton would move down the Susquehanna from Pennsylvania to the intersection of the Tioga River, while another, commanded by John Sullivan, Commander-in-Chief of the western troops, would ascend the valley.

The Indians fighting on both sides were far from unanimous in their loyalty and were pressured and coerced into giving support. The Mohawks, Senecas and Cayugas stayed with the British, while the Oneidas, some Onondagas, and Tuscaroras fought most often in support of the American colonists.

For a time the Oneidas were able to maintain a measure of neutrality. When Clinton and Sullivan prepared to crush the Indians on the frontiers, the Oneidas wavered and were about to throw in their lot with the Americans when Haldimand sent a stern warning and thinly veiled threat:

"For you will find that in case you slight or disregard this my last offer of peace, I shall soon convince you that I have such a number of Indian allies to let loose upon you, as will instantly convince you of your folly when too late, as I have hardly been able to restrain them from falling upon you for some time past."

Haldimand's warning did not go unheeded, for the Oneidas told Clinton:

"Brother: We suppose you imagine we have come here in order to attend you upon your expedition, but we are sorry to inform you that our situation is such as will not admit of it. From intelligence which we may depend upon, we have reason to believe that the Six Nations mean to embrace the opportunity of our absence in order to destroy our castles."

No amount of persuasion would change their minds but they did agree to send along one or two men as scouts.

Clinton went ahead with the plan and arrived at his destination with 5000 troops plus artillery and a corps of riflemen. With the utmost caution they advanced on Newtown, the present town of Elmira. There, behind extensive fortification, was a force estimated at 1500, including five companies of British troops and Rangers. Brant led the Indian troops and Colonel John Butler led the regulars and Rangers.

The Indians and Rangers gave a good account of

Sir Frederick Haldimand

themselves until an artillery bombardment and superior numbers turned their flank. Brant was everywhere, urging on his men and contesting each new position. His efforts were useless, however, and perceiving they were in danger of being surrounded, Indians and Rangers suddenly abandoned their defence works, crossed the river and fled. They were pursued for three kilometres and the bloody trail and abandoned equipment gave ample evidence of their disastrous and hasty retreat. The Americans burned and utterly destroyed all the houses, outbuildings, and cornfields.

The inhabitants of Newtown were only the first victims. Sullivan now went into action. He advanced through 41 Iroquois towns destroying all before him. Thousands of homeless, destitute Iroquois made their way to Fort Niagara where the English gave them refuge. Before leaving, Brant and the Mohawks buried their precious silver communion vessels in a barrel for safe-keeping during the war.

The devastation of their country by Sullivan and Clinton and their temporary encampment around Niagara meant terrible suffering from starvation and sickness for the Indian allies. To add to their misery, the winter of 1779-80 was one of the most severe on record. The entire New York frontier west of Schenectady was a smoking desert.

One of those most critical of Brant's policies and the resulting sufferings of his people was a Seneca chief Red Jacket, so named because of the military coat he always wore. He was a great orator and had considerable influence. Throughout his career he opposed Brant, and at this time of great hardship tried to arrange a separate peace between the Americans and the Six Nations. Brant, however, learned of the plot and scotched it.

Slowly the tide turned once more and Brant and his army, with the Rangers, struck again and again during 1780 at Harpersfield, Schoharie, Johnstown and Cana-joharie. By 1781 the Americans had ceased to offer much resistance in New York and Brant turned his attention to raids west to Detroit and as far south as Kentucky.

Peace Chapter 9

Effective and destructive as the frontier campaign had been, it was not decisive. The war was not going well for the British. France, Spain and the Netherlands had joined forces with the American colonists. Supplies and merchants were pouring in to help General Washington's beleaguered Continental Army. These reinforcements, combined with British bungling and underestimation of colonial strength and the Americans' determination to gain their independence, decided the outcome of the war.

Brant and his faithful Mohawks had expected the British defeat. They could see the futility of the battles they fought; it was obvious that the King's men were no longer invincible. On their last raid into the Mohawk country Brant had seen the destruction of Johnson Hall, Queen Anne's Chapel and his own home. He and Captain John Deseronto exhumed the communion silver and brought it back to Niagara.

The surrender of Lord Cornwallis, the British commander, at Yorktown on October 19, 1781, brought the war to an end and forced England to recognize the independence of the Thirteen Colonies. Now came the longer and harder job of winning the peace. Officially it was settled by the Treaty of Paris, signed on September 3, 1783, but it soon became apparent that the Indians had been forgotten. No provision was made for the return of the Iroquois lands to their rightful owners.

The United States boundaries had still to be settled, however, and the British held out hope by retaining possession of the western posts; Niagara, Oswego, Detroit and Michilimackinac. Brant saw clearly what he had to do: he must negotiate his own settlement and save what he could of the Iroquois heritage. Whatever the fate of the American colonies, King George had no right to cede the Indian lands to the colonists nor they to accept them. The French, and later the English, had occupied the chain of forts with the consent and support of the Iroquois, and the Treaty of Fort Stanwix in 1768 had confirmed the demarcation of Indian territory.

Lord Cornwallis, second-in-command of the British forces

Governor Haldimand realized the weakness of the British position and sent Colonel Guy Johnson to Niagara to try to placate the Indians who were growing more discontented and restless by the day. Haldimand had no desire for a repetition of the Pontiac uprising. But Brant was not content to deal with Johnson. Instead, he put on his British Army captain's dress uniform and headed by canoe for Quebec City and an audience with Haldimand himself.

When he presented himself at Haldimand's headquarters and demanded to see the governor, the duty officer frowned and declined. Brant, resplendent in his green coat with silver epaulettes, blue cloth leggings and breechcloth, the gorget of his captain's rank at his throat, and the eagle-feather cluster of a chief slanting back from his headdress, drew himself up to his full height and announced he was Joseph Brant. He was immediately ushered into Haldimand's presence.

Haldimand greeted him in a friendly manner. After commending Brant and his Mohawks for their loyal service he heard the war chief out. When Brant had finished his list of complaints and requests, which included restitution in land equivalent to that lost and for property losses, Haldimand asked if he would be prepared to settle in Canada.

Brant said that he had no choice since the Six Nations were unable to return to the United States, and requested permission for his people to settle by the Bay of Quinte, near Belleville on Lake Ontario. Finally, Haldimand agreed to send £15 000 and supplies of staple foods, the best the British government could do at the moment because of their obligations to the other Loyalists.

What sort of aid was Britain supplying to the Loyalists in Canada? Find out about other Loyalist settlements.

While in Quebec Brant met the Baron and Baroness Riedesel. Riedesel commanded a German contingent in the British Army during the war. His wife was very taken with "the famous Indian Chief, Captain Brant. His manners were polished: he expressed himself with fluency, and was much esteemed by General Haldimand. I dined once with him at the General's. In his dress he showed off to advantage the half military and half native costume. His countenance was manly and intelligent, and his disposition very mild."

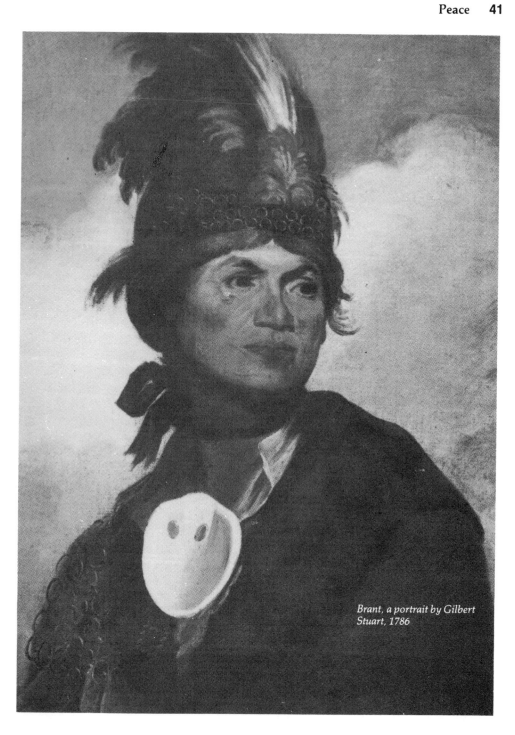

*Brant, a portrait by Gilbert
Stuart, 1786*

Despite invitations to remain in Quebec, Brant insisted on returning home as his people were anxious to know what had been agreed upon. Brant was happy at his success but on his return the Senecas criticized him. They objected that the Bay of Quinte was too far from their own lands, and suggested instead the area around the Grand River. And so on October 25, 1784, Haldimand signed a formal deed on behalf of George III ceding land on both sides of the Grand, ten kilometres wide from its source to its mouth on Lake Erie, "which they and their posterity are to enjoy forever."

Nevertheless, about 300 Mohawks including John Deseronto decided to settle around the Bay of Quinte. Deseronto's name was given to the village since he was the first to land there. The Quinte Indians insisted on their share of the heritage of the Mohawk — including half of Queen Anne's communion silver. Brant, however, retained the leather-bound Bible for his new settlement at Brantford. This name came from "Brant's Ford," the crossing Brant made across the shallows of the Grand.

Some Cayugas, Onondagas, Tuscaroras and Senecas joined the Mohawks on the Grand River. Bark shelters served until a sawmill was erected to provide lumber for wooden floors and shingle roofs. Soon they added a church, a school and a longhouse for a council chamber. The land on the Grand River had not been surveyed and there were conflicting claims to be dealt with. Brant's policy of selling portions of the grant to provide

Haldimand's deed granting land to the Indians of the Six Nations on both sides of the Grand River

necessary supplies for the new settlers was also criticized. Nevertheless by 1784-85, more than 1500 Indians had moved into the area around the new settlement.

The first years were difficult, especially 1787, widely known as the "Hungry Year." Fields of corn and other vegetables withered, streams and wells ran dry, and game was hard to find. The Indians supplemented their

Brant and the Mohawks at Grand River

meagre provisions with berries, edible roots and fish caught with their hands in the now shallow stretches of the Grand.

During this first decade Brant's lot was not an easy one nor was it made easier by the new Lieutenant-Governor, John Graves Simcoe. While Simcoe was generally friendly and even visited Brant and his new settlement, he suspected Brant of planning to create an independent Iroquois nation.

In 1782, Brant had received a Loyalist grant of land on Burlington Bay, Lake Ontario, for his own home. He had built a compact house on it which he called Wellington Square. His family life was divided between this house and another in the Grand Valley. But as his land policies came under severe and increasing attack not only from the government but from a faction among his own people, he determined to attempt further negotiations in England and the United States to improve their lot.

John Graves Simcoe

Chapter 10 Futile Negotiations

Why was Brant unable to unite the tribes?

Already in September 1783 the Indians of the Northwest and the South were in a state of unrest. Delegates of the Miamis, Delawares, Hurons, Wyandots, Potawatamis, the confederated tribes along the Wabash, the Chippewas from the north, Cherokees, Crees, and Shawnees from the south, met Brant and representatives of the Six Nations at Sandusky.

Brant held a place of honour in the council circle and made a strong plea for Indian unity which had been his dream for many years. The King's representative urged them to accept new territory, but Brant and a delegation were sent with their petition to Fort Stanwix to meet with the American commissioners.

Governor Clinton of New York tried to prevent Brant's meeting with the federal commissioners sent by General Washington to arrange an amicable settlement. Clinton had no intention of returning the Iroquois lands. General Schuyler made a deliberately aggressive speech with derogatory remarks about the "Four Nations," as he insisted on calling them. By 1784 it was obvious to all the Indians that neither the Americans nor the British were prepared to retain the lands between the Ohio and Lake Ontario for the Iroquois. The Indian dream of an all-Indian confederacy was destroyed, and Chief Red Jacket and Chief Cornplanter (also a Seneca) were left to argue the best course for the western Indian. Against the wishes of Red Jacket, Cornplanter concluded a treaty with the Americans, which defined the boundaries of their land. Under the terms of the pact, the Americans demanded not only the return of all prisoners of war but six Indian hostages as a guarantee of good faith. One of the hostages was Aaron Hill, a Mohawk chief.

Furious at this treaty and unhappy with his inability to sell the lands of the Indian grant in the Grand Valley when necessary, Brant prepared to appeal directly to the

Brant, painted by
William Berczy (1744-
1813). Find out more
about Berczy who was
one of the founders
of Toronto, Ontario.

King. At the end of 1785, he sailed for England. He was royally received and entertained by such notable personalities as Lord Percy and the Earl of Warwick. Lord Moira gave him his picture set in gold and Charles James Fox presented him with a silver snuffbox engraved with Brant's initials. He was equally welcome in the Prince of Wales' circle and enjoyed an association with Burke and Sheridan, British political figures of the age.

One evening Brant was invited to a fancy dress ball. He came, at the request of Lord Moira, wearing no mask but with one half of his face painted, and his rich robes cinched by a belt in which his burnished tomahawk glittered. Also at the ball was a Turkish diplomat who, intrigued by Brant's costume and thinking he was wearing a mask, tweaked his nose. Brant, seeing the humour of the situation decided to have a little fun of his own. He let loose a blood-curdling war cry, drew his tomahawk and whirled it manacingly over the terror-stricken Turk. The women shrieked and scurried for cover while the diplomat stood trembling but riveted to the spot. The incident was soon explained and the gaiety of the ball resumed.

Having received the King's promise of compensation, Brant returned to the Grand in 1786 only to become involved once more in negotiations. First he met with the western Indians in another attempt at unity. They drafted a conciliatory proposal for presentation to the American government. The Americans, however, decided on a policy of "divide and conquer" and in 1789, General St. Clair made two separate treaties with the Five Nations (Mohawks excepted) and with the Wyandots, Delawares, Ottawas, Chippewas, Potawatomis and Sac nations. St. Clair wrote, "I am persuaded their general confederacy is entirely broken. Indeed it would not be very difficult... to set them at deadly variance." Brant's attempts at uniting the Indian tribes were at an end.

Despite the treaties, the Shawnees, Miamis, and Wabash kept up a bloody war with the Kentucky settlements. All attempts to negotiate having failed, General Harmer advanced on the Indians in 1790 with 1300 Kentucky and Pennsylvanian troops, only to suffer a humiliating defeat. This success naturally emboldened the Indians, and they carried the war into Ohio and

Pennsylvania. The invaders appealed to Haldimand and Brant for help from the British and the Mohawks, but they were unwilling to engage in a war against the United States at this time.

In 1791, General St. Clair and 1400 men made another attempt to subdue the Indians, only to meet the same humiliation as General Harmer. The Americans lost 38 officers and 493 non-commissioned officers and men. In addition, the Indians acquired, besides numerous rifles, muskets and other equipment, eight field-guns and 400 horses. The acknowledged leader of this Indian resistance was Little Turtle, a distinguished chief of the Miamis. It was suspected, however, that the mastermind behind the scenes was none other than Joseph Brant.

The Americans now feared that this second success would encourage the Five Nations to carry on the war in alliance with the western tribes. It was time for drastic action and in response to the anguished cries of the frontiersmen, George Washington, President of the United States, appointed General Anthony Wayne to lead yet another expedition.

A sketch of a Mohawk village on the Grand River, from the diary of Mrs. John Graves Simcoe

While this expeditionary force was being prepared, final attempts were made to secure a peaceful settlement. Fifty Iroquois sachems including Cornplanter were invited to Philadelphia. Brant received a special invitation to meet Washington there. At first he refused, but arrived on June 20, 1792 and was received with marked attention.

He received more than attention: "I was offered a thousand guineas down, and to have the half-pay and pension I receive from Great Britain doubled, merely on condition that I would use my endeavours to bring about a peace. But this I rejected." The Americans then increased the bribe to the equivalent of $100 000 in land and $1 500 a year. But all they got was Brant's promise to do what he could to persuade the Miamis and other warring tribes to make peace.

Brant, Cornplanter, and the other peacemakers were unsuccessful. The Miamis and Shawnees insisted on the boundary agreed upon at the Treaty of Fort Stanwix. Anything short of that would mean continuation of hostilities.

When the negotiations failed, Wayne moved against the hostile Indians. The first skirmish near Fort Recovery resulted in an Indian defeat. Wayne then proceeded cautiously with a force of about 2000 men against a similar number of Indians under Little Turtle near Fort Miami.

A bayonet charge by the infantry and a cavalry pursuit with sabres gave Wayne a decisive victory at the Battle of Fallen Timbers in August 1794. The Indian losses were substantial and never again would they be a threat to the western frontier. Grenville's·Treaty in 1795 surrendered the western posts to the United States. The far-western Indians recrossed the Mississippi, convinced that further resistance was useless.

The Mohawk Chapel

Joseph Brant returned to the Grand Valley a disappointed man, for the dream of an all-Indian Confederacy was shattered. He now sought comfort in his strong religious faith and in the completion of the church, begun in 1785, which would afford his people similar consolation.

Have the treaties with Indian tribes been fair?

The building, twenty metres long and fourteen metres wide, had been built of squared logs, boarded on the outside and painted. Above it rose a spire and bell tower which served as a landmark for all the surrounding area. In the tower hung a huge bell cast in England, a gift of the British government.

The Gospel according to St. John, published in Mohawk and English in 1804. The Gospel according to St. Mark was similarly printed in both languages.

(14)

n'oghwhenjàge ok yaghten tesewcghtaghkon, ogh-
nen-awen aontcseweghtaghkon nene enkwaghrory
tsinikarrihhoten ne Karonyàge?

13 Yagh onghka n'ongwe encken teyakawe-
nonghton Karonyàge ok ne raonha n'egh thoyengh-
taghkwen ne Karonyage ne naah ne rongwe ronwa-
yeah ne ne Karonyage yehenideron.

14 Ok tsiniyought ne Moses t'hoketikwen n'on-
yàre karhagon, etho oni nen yàwenne n'ongwe ron-
waye-ah enhonwaketikwen.

15 Nene onghka kiok teyakaweghtaghkon raonhage yaghten a-onghtonde ok rodiyen ne eterna
adonheta.

16 Iken ne Yehovah egh ne s'hakonoronghàwa
n'ongwe, nene rodewendeghton nene raonhaon rodewedon rohhàwak, nene onghka kiok teyaka-
weghdaghkon raonhage yaghten a-onghtonde, ok
denghton aontehodiyendane ne eterna adonheta.

17 Iken Niyoh yaghten yehonha-on ne royea-h
n'oghwhentjàge ongweghne nene enshakedewen-
deghte n'ongwe, ok nene aontyesenhak raonha
raoriwa n'ongwe enshonwadiyàdagon.

18 Raonha nene tehhaweghtaghkon raonhage
yaghten enhonwadewenndeght, ok raonha nene
yaghten tehaweghtaghkon a onen si rogwadewenn-
deghton, ne wahhòni tsi yaghfen tehaweghtaghkon ne raoghiénagon ne raonha-on rodewedon
rohhàwak ne Yehovah.

(14)

believe not, how shall ye believe if I tell you of
heavenly things?

13 And no man hath ascended up to heaven
but he that came down from heaven, even the Son
of man, which is in heaven,

14 And as Moses lifted up the serpent in the
wilderness, even so must the Son of man be lifted
up:

15 That whosoever believeth in him should not
perish, but have eternal life.

16 For God so loved the world, that he gave his
only begotten Son, that whosoever believeth in him
should not perish, but have everlasting life.

17 For God sent not his Son into the world to
condemn the world, but that the world through
him might be saved.

18 He that believeth on him is not condemned:
but he that believeth not is condemned already,
because he hath not believed in the name of the
only begotten Son of God.

The Mohawks' share of the
Queen Anne silver communion
service

Inside were pews made of boards joined by wooden pegs. On the lectern was Queen Anne's leather-bound Bible, which had been salvaged from the Mohawk Valley, while the silver vessels rested on the communion table. The pulpit was flanked by two tablets in the Mohawk language: the Lord's Prayer and the Ten Commandments. Over the door was the royal coat-of-arms carved in wood and lacquered in red, blue and gold.

Everything was now ready for the dedication. Brant and four other chiefs paddled to Cataraqui (now Kingston), to ask the Reverend John Stuart to perform the consecration service. With other Loyalists, Stuart had fled across Lake Ontario to Fort Frontenac where he became chaplain to the garrison. He gladly accepted the invitation and embarked in Brant's canoe on the nine-day, 320 kilometre journey to Burlington. There they were met by an escort on horseback who followed a now well-defined trail back to Brant's Ford.

On a brilliant Sunday, in June 1788 the great bell boomed out its call to the service of dedication. The Indians of the district came in great numbers, by canoe, others on horseback or on foot. Each person was handed a book containing the Prayer Books, Psaltery, and the Gospel according to St. Mark, which Brant had translated into the Mohawk language and which he had had published in London on his last visit.

Brant led the chaplain down the sloping path from his house, across the bridge and through the white picket fence which surrounded the chapel, up to the door which then faced the river.

The chapel was filled to overflowing. The Indians sang the opening hymn with great enthusiasm and listened attentively to the sermon. The dedication was followed by a service in which 65 people were baptised; three couples were married. The congregation had to take advantage of the visit of an ordained minister to perform these rites as another might not come their way for several months, or perhaps even years in the more remote areas. Most ministers at that time were itinerant missionaries who travelled on horseback over the vast areas that were their charges.

The Indians at Brant's Ford attended their own services faithfully each Sunday, even without a minister.

Unable to persuade Mr. Stuart to stay with the
Mohawks, Brant made determined efforts to find a
minister for his people. He had been promised one by
the King himself during his visit with George III who
personally appealed to the Archbishop of Canterbury
and the Society for the Propagation of the Gospel.

When a missionary was not forthcoming, Brant fixed
on Davenport Phelps, whom he had known during the
Revolutionary War and who had married the daughter
of the Reverand Eleazer Wheelock. In 1792, Phelps visited
Upper Canada and received a grant of 42 000 hectares of
land from Governor Simcoe. He settled in Niagara where
he practised law and established a printing office.

Despite representations from Brant, the British
bishops refused to accept Phelps as a candidate for holy
orders. Brant then appealed to the bishops of the United

States and Phelps was ordained deacon in Trinity
Church, New York, by Bishop Benjamin Moore on Sunday, December 13, 1801. He was ordained priest in St.
Peter's, Albany, by the same bishop the following year
and subsequently settled in Upper Canada. He, too,
declined to live in the remote areas despite Brant's
entreaties, preferring to discharge his duties around
Burlington Bay. There, Brant was occasionally in his
congregation and listened eagerly to his sermons.

In the meantime Brant continued his work of trans-
lating the Bible into Mohawk, a work which would long
outlive him and which showed his appreciation of
biblical language and its poetry.

The final tribute came in 1904 when the King desig-
nated Brant's church as "His Majesty's Chapel to the
Mohawks," one of the few royal chapels in the world.

Cataraqui at the time the royal chapel was dedicated

The Mohawk Chapel at Brantford, as Brant knew it

The Closing Years

Brant continued to struggle with successive governors and superintendents of Indian affairs over the Indians' right to dispose of their land as they saw fit.

In 1793, Lieutenant-Governor Simcoe issued a new deed: the land belonged to the Indians only so long as they remained on it. If at any time they left, it would revert to the Crown. They were not able to sell or transfer it to others.

Brant protested that this was contrary to the Haldimand agreement and carried the case to Lord Dorchester, Governor of Upper and Lower Canada, and Simcoe's superior. As the two men, Simcoe and Dorchester, tended to disagree on most matters, Dorchester supported Brant's contention but he, in turn, was overruled by the British government.

Brant renewed his application to Simcoe's successor, the Honourable Peter Russell, and was jubilant when in 1797 the Executive Council of Upper Canada, meeting at York (Toronto), agreed to comply with the Indians' request to allow them to dispose of some of their land. Brant's high hopes were again dashed, however, when the British Home Secretary refused to endorse the Council's decision.

Despite these manoeuverings, by 1798, approximately 15 000 hectares of of the original grant of 290 000 hectares had been sold. But Brant's claim that the Indians had the right to dispose of their lands as they wished was not finally settled until the mid-nineteenth century, long after his death.

How were Iroquois land claims finally settled? Have all native land claims been settled by now?

Nor did Brant's enemies stop at blocking his attempts to dispose of the land. They accused Brant of using the money so obtained for his own purposes. The leader of this dissident element was none other than his old enemy Chief Red Jacket. When they dared to accuse him to his face of the misappropriation of some $38 000 and informed him they had deposed him as war chief of the Six Nations, he heaped scorn on them, called them traitors, and with his hand on his tomahawk drove them from his house.

In Brantford, Joseph's loyal people acted quickly and reaffirmed their trust and devotion. Sixteen chiefs signed a document of confidence in his leadership and runners were dispatched to inform the far reaches of the settlement. Red Jacket's treachery had failed and Brant's leadership henceforth was unchallenged.

This attempt to depose him was not the only bitterness he had to endure in his old age. Each year the Six Nations gathered at Wellington Square, Brant's home on Burlington Bay, to receive their annual bounty from the government consisting of clothing and trinkets. In 1795 this occasion was marred by a tragic incident.

Isaac Brant, Joseph Brant's oldest son by his first

CAMROSE LUTHERAN COLLEGE
LIBRARY

The Honourable Peter Russell,
painted by William Berczy

wife, had always had a bad character. He grew more hateful as time went on, and jealousy of his seven half-brothers and -sisters by Brant's third wife added to his unpleasant traits. He never ceased to heap abuse on his stepmother and showed open hostility to his father; in fact, he was often found in the ranks of Brant's enemies.

Brant not only did not return this hatred but continued to show his son exceptional love and understanding. Isaac drank heavily and could become completely uncontrollable. On two occasions he ran afoul of the law, once by mutilating a traveller and another time by murdering a man.

After the murder he threatened to kill his father in the inn where both were lodged. When Brant entered Isaac's room in an attempt to quieten his violent outburst, Isaac lunged at him with a knife, severely cutting the back of Brant's hand. Brant, in self-defence, struck back with his dirk, lacerating Isaac's scalp.

Brant sent for a nearby doctor and had Isaac's wound treated and dressed but Isaac, mad with rage and drink, tore the bandages off. Subsequently the wound became infected, and within days Isaac was dead.

Brant was heartbroken and conscience-stricken by the death of his favourite and first-born by his own hand. He turned himself over to the authorities for judgement and submitted his resignation. Isaac's death was ruled justified homicide. The Indian Council also acquitted Brant of all blame.

In spite of this and the universal sympathy he received, Brant's conscience would not let him rest and he often wept in his own room gazing at the dagger that killed his son. It was a sorrow he was to carry with him to his grave.

As Brant grew older, he withdrew more and more from active participation in negotiations and Indian affairs generally. As he withdrew, his adopted nephew Captain John Norton (Teyoninhokaraven) became prominent among the Mohawks.

Norton was of mixed blood, his father Indian and his mother a Scotswoman. Next to Brant he was the most distinguished of modern Mohawks. When Brant was no longer able to travel far, Norton acted as his business agent and representative. One of these trips took Norton to Britain to argue Brant's land claims with the British government.

Norton laid Brant's case in strong and lucid language before the King's ministers. He argued that Indian lands should be free of all encumbrances and that if this were done Upper Canada (Ontario) would be further strengthened by the immigration of a major part of the tribes of the Six Nations still resident in the United States. Obviously this was a revival of Brant's old dream of bringing together the Indian Confederacy as one nation.

When his proposal was rejected by the British, Brant contemplated withdrawing completely from Canada and he sent Norton to treat with Governor Jay of New York State. The legislators of New York were not willing to relinquish large tracts of land around Lake Champlain which members of the confederacy were claiming. After this, Brant withdrew from the struggle and settled down in his home in Burlington.

When Joseph Brant died in November 1807, the choice of his successor was, by Iroquois tradition, the sole right of his third wife Catherine. She could have chosen John Norton, but her choice was her fourth and youngest son John, Ahyouwaigha.

The young new chief had been born at the Mohawk Village on September 27, 1794. He received a good English education and improved this basic knowledge by continued study and travel.

When the War of 1812 between the United States and England broke out, John Brant threw in his lot with the forces of the King and took part in all the major battles. By doing this he remained true to the ancient Mohawk tradition and large numbers of his nation followed his lead.

When the war ended in 1815, he made his home at the head of the lake, living in the English style and dispensing the same generous hospitality as his father had. Visitors spoke of him as "a fine young man of gentlemanly appearance who used the English language with precision and correctness, and who dressed in English style except for his moccasins."

In 1821, John Brant journeyed to England in the same cause as his father before him. As a result, in 1822 the Secretary for the Colonies, Lord Bathurst, asked Sir Peregine Maitland, then governor of Upper Canada, to redress the Indian grievances. Although Brant had won his spurs as a successful diplomat, once more the efforts of the local politicians thwarted his hopes.

In 1827, Brant was promoted to the rank of captain and appointed superintendent of the Six Nations. Five years later he was returned as a member of the provincial parliament for the county of Haldimand. In the same year, however, he died of cholera. Thus ended the promising career of Joseph Brant's son.

Chapter 13 **After Brant**

What is your opinion of Joseph Brant's motives and deeds?

Brant left behind him a controversial reputation and a variety of accomplishments which have lasted to this day.

Accusations of violence plague his name, although many of these accusations have been disproven. He is remembered with bitterness by the families of those who survived his raids in the Mohawk Valley.

Even among his own people opinion is divided. From the beginning of their life in Canada, the values of the Iroquois refugees were split. His attempts to sell or trade off land grants have been misunderstood, and he has been labelled a scoundrel because of them.

Yet he has many loyal supporters too. Memorials and statues attest to his achievements, and the Thayendanegea Reserve (between Kingston and Belleville, Ontario) is named after him.

Mohawk legend says Brant dreamt in his youth that he would wear the Magic Moccasins, meaning that he would lead his people. This he certainly did to the best of his ability, but he and all the Iroquois were caught in the whirlpool of two opposing cultural currents. He was powerless against the diseases and liquor the settlers brought with them, which had such harmful effects on the native people. Nor could he prevent the expansion of Europeans into lands where the Iroquois once held sway.

The place of Joseph Brant in history is secured by his statesmanship and his unquestionable loyalty to the British. The aid he and his troops provided during the Revolutionary War was crucial in allowing the British to maintain a dominion in the larger part of North America.

Brant's work provided a bridge between Europe and the New World. For all his loyalty to Britain, Brant remained a Mohawk, and made sure his people would be allowed to retain their distinct culture as well.

Brant towards the end of his life

Further Reading

Elliott, J.L. (ed.) *Native Peoples*. Toronto: Prentice-Hall, 1971.

Feder, Norman. *Two Hundred Years of North American Indian Art*. New York: Praeger, 1972.

Flexner, James T. *Mohawk Baronet — Sir William Johnson of New York*. New York: Harper Bros., 1959.

Monture, Ethel Brant. "Joseph Brant," *Famous Indians*. Toronto: Clarke, Irwin, 1960.

Neering, Rosemary. *Life of the Loyalists*. Toronto: Fitzhenry & Whiteside, 1975.

Robinson, Helen C. *Joseph Brant — A Man for His People*. Toronto: Longman, 1971.

Surtees, Robert J. *The Original People*. Toronto: Holt, Rinehart and Winston, 1971.

Symington, Fraser. *The Canadian Indian*. Toronto: McClelland & Stewart, 1969.

Widdemar, Margaret. *The Lady of the Mohawks* (Molly Brant). New York: Doubleday, 1951.

Credits

The author would like to recognize the assistance afforded to him in the preparation of this book by Mrs. Sheila Wilson of the St. Catharines Public Library; Mr. James Hogan, Librarian of Brock University; Mr. Harold Calderwood, Curator of the Johnstown Historical Society; the Reverend Canon Zimmerman of the Mohawk Chapel, Brantford; Mr. Carroll Lewis, Curator Of Wellington Square, Burlington; Mr. Samuel Canavan, Curator of Fort Johnson; and Chief Melville Hill of Deseronto.

The publishers wish to express their gratitude to the following who have given permission to use copyrighted illustrations in this book:

The Trustees of the British Museum London, England, page 29.

Dartmouth College Museum and Galleries, Hanover, New Hampshire, page 19.

The Hurley Printing Company Limited, Brantford, Ontario, pages 42, 51.

The Hudson's Bay Company, Winnipeg, pages 4, 6.

The Metropolitan Toronto Library Board, pages 13, 20, 26, 33, 45, 58.

The National Gallery of Canada, frontispiece, page 30, 47.

Courtesy of the New York State Historical Association, Cooperstown, pages 41, 63.

Praeger Pubs., New York, page 8.

Public Archives of Canada, pages 16 (C24852), 17 (C2712), 27 (C6150), 37 (C3221), 39 (C11070), 44 (IF-20), 49, 54 (C1511), 56 (C70361).

Public Archives of Ontario, page 59.

Editors: Laura Damania, Barbara Czarnecki

Every effort has been made to credit all sources correctly. The author and publishers will welcome any information that will allow them to correct any errors or omissions.